INTRODUCTION	2
BANANA QUILT	4
BIRTHDAY CAKE QUILT	8
BUTTERED PECAN QUILT	12
COCONUT QUILT	16
COFFEE QUILT	20
COOKIE DOUGH QUILT	24
COOKIES 'N CREAM QUILT	28
COTTON CANDY QUILT	32
DUTCH CHOCOLATE QUILT	36
FRENCH VANILLA QUILT	40
LEMON SORBET QUILT	44
MINT CHOCOLATE CHIP QUILT	48
NEAPOLITAN QUILT	52
PEACHES 'N CREAM QUILT	56
RAINBOW SHERBET QUILT	60
ROCKY ROAD QUILT	64

Front cover quilt features Little Snippets by Bonnie & Camille for Moda Fabrics.

PERFECT 10 QUILTS

Introduction

Terrific 10" Squares

It's no secret that precuts have become a beloved staple in the quilting world. They can be used in many ways to make spectacular quilts while saving precious time, and the 10" square is no exception. Most commonly called a Layer Cake®, named by Moda Fabrics who pioneered this precut, it can also be found under names like 10" Squares, Stackers, Crackers and more. This precut typically contains a 10" square of each print in a fabric collection and sometimes includes duplicates of some prints.

Lots of sizes and shapes can be cut from a 10" square and combined for an infinite number of designs, which leads us to the Perfect 10 Ruler for your 10" squares!

Perfect 10 Quilts

It may sound like these cut sizes will only take you so far, but the 16 fabulous quilts in this book beg to differ. Using 10" squares, the Perfect 10 Ruler and simple piecing techniques, you can achieve a versatile range of looks and styles. They are all simple and simply wonderful!

What are you waiting for? Start by picking up the Creative Grids Perfect 10 Ruler at your favorite quilt store and gather up the 10" squares in your sewing room (time for some serious stashbusting). Then grab your rotary cutter and get ready for some sensationally sweet cutting and piecing for a super satisfying quilt!

WOF = width of fabric

¼" seams and press as arrows indicate throughout

Introduction

Creative Grids Perfect 10 Ruler

The Perfect 10 Ruler, designed by It's Sew Emma for Creative Grids®, was designed to unlock the true potential of 10" squares. This 10" square ruler has been simplified to help you quickly and accurately cut fabric into just the sizes you need.

10" squares are perfect to cut into 2 ½", 5" and 9 ½" squares and rectangles. These cut widths go together like a charm, and the Perfect 10 Ruler makes the cutting a cinch. You can also use this ruler to easily trim down half square triangles and other pieced units to just the right size.

Cutting 2 ½" rectangles
Use the dashed 2 ½" line to cut four 2 ½" rectangles.

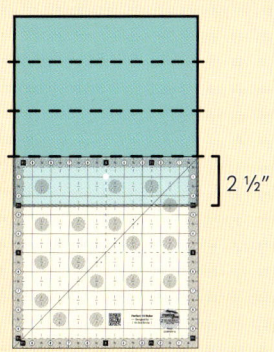

Cutting 5" rectangles
Use the solid 5" line to cut two 5" rectangles.

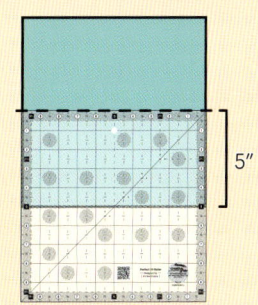

Trim Half Square Triangles
Align the diagonal seam of the oversized unit with the 45° line and the desired unfinished size. Cut along the outside edge of the ruler.

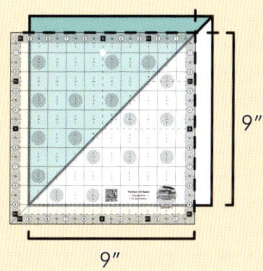

Cutting 2 ½" squares
Follow the instructions above to cut four 2 ½" rectangles. Then, use the dashed 2 ½" line to subcut into sixteen 2 ½" squares.

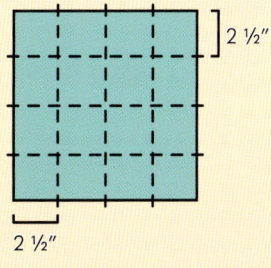

Cutting 5" squares
Follow the instructions above to cut two 5" rectangles. Then, use the solid 5" line to subcut into four 5" squares.

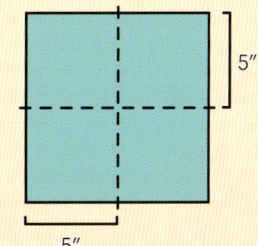

Cutting 9 ½" squares
Use the dashed 9 ½" line to cut one 9 ½" rectangle. Then, use the dashed 9 ½" line to subcut into one 9 ½" square.

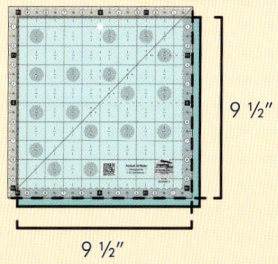

Banana Quilt

65" x 65"

CUTTING INSTRUCTIONS:

One Layer Cake (36 - 10" squares)	
Blocks 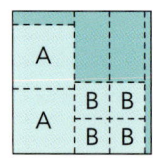	From each 10" square cut: 2 - 4 ½" squares (A) 4 - 2 ½" squares (B)

3 ⅓ yards	
Background, Sashing & Borders	9 - 4 ½" x WOF strips, subcut into: 72 - 4 ½" squares (C)
	10 - 2" x WOF strips, subcut into: 9 - 2" x 18" rectangles (D) 18 - 2" x 8 ½" rectangles (E)
	3 - 3 ½" x WOF strips, subcut into: 6 - 3 ½" x 18" rectangles (F)
	11 - 3 ½" x WOF strips, sew end to end and subcut into: 2 - 3 ½" x 59" strips (G1) 2 - 3 ½" x 59" strips (G2) 2 - 3 ½" x 65" strips (G3)

¾ yard	
Binding	8 - 2 ½" x WOF strips (H)

| 4 ¼ yards Backing | |

Banana Quilt

BANANA BLOCKS:

Each Block uses four 10" squares (set).

Draw a diagonal line on the wrong side of the Fabric B squares.

With right sides facing, layer a Fabric B square on the top right corner of a Fabric C square.

Stitch on the drawn line and trim ¼" away from the seam.

Repeat on the bottom left corner with matching fabric.

Partial Banana Unit should measure 4 ½" x 4 ½".

Make two from each 10" square.
Make seventy-two total.

Assemble Unit using matching fabric.
Banana Unit should measure 8 ½" x 8 ½".

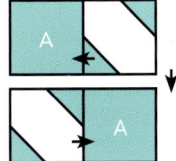 

Make one from each 10" square.
Make thirty-six total.

Assemble Block using coordinating fabric.
Banana Block should measure 18" x 18".

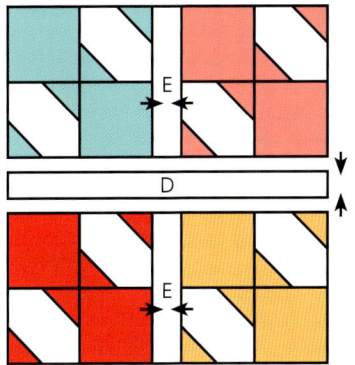 

Make one from each set.
Make nine total.

PERFECT 10 QUILTS 5

Banana Quilt

QUILT CENTER:

Assemble Quilt Center. Press toward the Fabric F rectangles.

Quilt Center should measure 59" x 59".

BORDERS:

Attach the Side Borders using the Fabric G2 strips.

Attach the Top and Bottom Borders using the Fabric G3 strips.

FINISHING:

Piece the Fabric H strips end to end for binding.

Quilt and bind as desired.

Birthday Cake Quilt

66 ½" x 66 ½"

CUTTING INSTRUCTIONS:

One Layer Cake (36 - 10" squares)	
Blocks 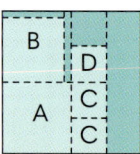	From each 10" square cut: 1 - 5" square (A) 1 - 4 ½" square (B) 2 - 2 ½" squares (C) 1 - 2 ½" square (D) *

3 ⅝ yards	
Background, Sashing & Borders	5 - 5" x WOF strips, subcut into: 36 - 5" squares (E)
	5 - 4 ½" x WOF strips, subcut into: 36 - 4 ½" squares (F)
	15 - 2 ½" x WOF strips, subcut into: 60 - 2 ½" x 8 ½" rectangles (G)
	8 - 4 ½" x WOF strips, sew end to end and subcut into: 2 - 4 ½" x 58 ½" strips (H1) 2 - 4 ½" x 66 ½" strips (H2)

¾ yard	
Binding	8 - 2 ½" x WOF strips (I)

4 ¼ yards Backing	

* You will not use all Fabric D squares.

Birthday Cake Quilt

BIRTHDAY CAKE BLOCKS:

Draw a diagonal line on the wrong side of the Fabric E squares.

With right sides facing, layer a Fabric E square with a Fabric A square.

Stitch ¼" from each side of the drawn line.

Cut apart on the marked line.

TRIM Half Square Triangle Unit to measure 4 ½" x 4 ½".

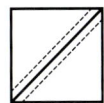  

Make two from each 10" square.

Make seventy-two total.

Draw a diagonal line on the wrong side of the Fabric C squares.

With right sides facing, layer a Fabric C square on the top left corner of a Fabric F square.

Stitch on the drawn line and trim ¼" away from the seam.

Repeat on the bottom right corner with matching fabric.

Birthday Cake Unit should measure 4 ½" x 4 ½".

Make one from each 10" square.

Make thirty-six total.

Assemble Block using matching fabric.

Birthday Cake Block should measure 8 ½" x 8 ½".

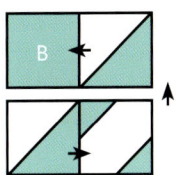 

Make one from each 10" square.

Make thirty-six total.

PERFECT 10 QUILTS

Birthday Cake Quilt

QUILT CENTER:

Assemble Quilt Center. Press toward the Fabric G rectangles.

Quilt Center should measure 58 ½" x 58 ½".

Birthday Cake Quilt

BORDERS:

Attach the Side Borders using the Fabric H1 strips.

Attach the Top and Bottom Borders using the Fabric H2 strips.

FINISHING:

Piece the Fabric I strips end to end for binding.

Quilt and bind as desired.

PERFECT 10 QUILTS

Buttered Pecan Quilt

78 ½" x 78 ½"

CUTTING INSTRUCTIONS:

One Layer Cake (36 - 10" squares)	
Blocks 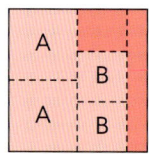	From each 10" square cut: 2 - 5" squares (A) 2 - 3 ½" squares (B)

5 ¼ yards	
Background & Borders	9 - 5" x WOF strips, subcut into: 72 - 5" squares (C)
	9 - 4 ½" x WOF strips, subcut into: 72 - 4 ½" squares (D)
	24 - 2 ½" x WOF strips, subcut into: 72 - 2 ½" x 12 ½" rectangles (E)
	9 - 3 ½" x WOF strips, sew end to end and subcut into: 2 - 3 ½" x 72 ½" strips (F1) 2 - 3 ½" x 78 ½" strips (F2)

⅞ yard	
Binding	9 - 2 ½" x WOF strips (G)

| 7 ⅜ yards Backing | |

Buttered Pecan Quilt

BUTTERED PECAN BLOCKS:

Each Block uses two 10" squares (pair).

Draw a diagonal line on the wrong side of the Fabric C squares.

With right sides facing, layer a Fabric C square with a Fabric A square.

Stitch ¼" from each side of the drawn line.

Cut apart on the marked line.

TRIM Half Square Triangle Unit to measure 4 ½" x 4 ½".

 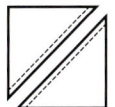 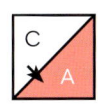

Make four from each 10" square.

Make one hundred forty-four total.

Draw a diagonal line on the wrong side of the Fabric B squares.

With right sides facing, layer a Fabric B square on the top right corner of a Fabric D square.

Stitch on the drawn line and trim ¼" away from the seam.

Partial Buttered Pecan Unit should measure 4 ½" x 4 ½".

Make two from each 10" square.

Make seventy-two total.

Assemble Unit using coordinating fabric.

Buttered Pecan Unit should measure 8 ½" x 12 ½".

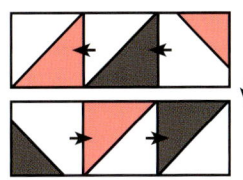 

Make two from each pair.

Make thirty-six total.

Assemble Block.

Buttered Pecan Block should measure 12 ½" x 12 ½".

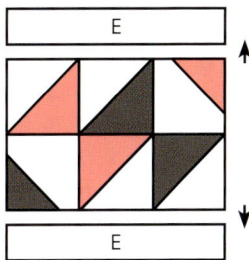 

Make two from each pair.

Make thirty-six total.

PERFECT 10 QUILTS

Buttered Pecan Quilt

QUILT CENTER:

Assemble Quilt Center. Press rows in opposite directions.

Quilt Center should measure 72 ½" x 72 ½".

Buttered Pecan Quilt

BORDERS:

Attach the Side Borders using the Fabric F1 strips.

Attach the Top and Bottom Borders using the Fabric F2 strips.

FINISHING:

Piece the Fabric G strips end to end for binding.

Quilt and bind as desired.

Coconut Quilt

63" x 63"

CUTTING INSTRUCTIONS:

One Layer Cake (36 - 10" squares)	
Blocks	From each 10" square cut: 2 - 4 ½" squares (A) 8 - 2" squares (B) 1 - 1 ½" square (C)

3 ⅔ yards	
Background, Sashing & Borders	9 - 4 ½" x WOF strips, subcut into: 72 - 4 ½" squares (D)
	15 - 1 ½" x WOF strips, subcut into: 144 - 1 ½" x 4" rectangles (E)
	8 - 2" x WOF strips, subcut into: 30 - 2" x 8 ½" rectangles (F)
	8 - 2" x WOF strips, sew end to end and subcut into: 5 - 2" x 56" strips (G)
	7 - 4" x WOF strips, sew end to end and subcut into: 2 - 4" x 56" strips (H1) 2 - 4" x 63" strips (H2)

¾ yard	
Binding	8 - 2 ½" x WOF strips (I)

| 4 ⅛ yards Backing | |

PERFECT 10 QUILTS

COCONUT BLOCKS:

Draw a diagonal line on the wrong side of the Fabric D squares.

With right sides facing, layer a Fabric D square with a Fabric A square.

Stitch ¼" from each side of the drawn line.

Cut apart on the marked line.

TRIM Half Square Triangle Unit to measure 4" x 4".

Make four from each 10" square.

Make one hundred forty-four total.

Draw a diagonal line on the wrong side of the Fabric B squares.

With right sides facing, layer a Fabric B square on the top right corner of a matching Half Square Triangle Unit.

Stitch on the drawn line and trim ¼" away from the seam.

Repeat on the bottom left corner with matching fabric.

Coconut Unit should measure 4" x 4".

Make four from each 10" square.

Make one hundred forty-four total.

Assemble Block using matching fabric.

Coconut Block should measure 8 ½" x 8 ½".

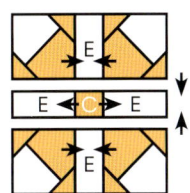 

Make one from each 10" square.

Make thirty-six total.

PERFECT 10 QUILTS

Coconut Quilt

QUILT CENTER:

Assemble Quilt Center. Press toward the Fabric F rectangles.

Quilt Center should measure 56" x 56".

Coconut Quilt

BORDERS:

Attach the Side Borders using the Fabric H1 strips.

Attach the Top and Bottom Borders using the Fabric H2 strips.

FINISHING:

Piece the Fabric I strips end to end for binding.

Quilt and bind as desired.

Coffee Quilt

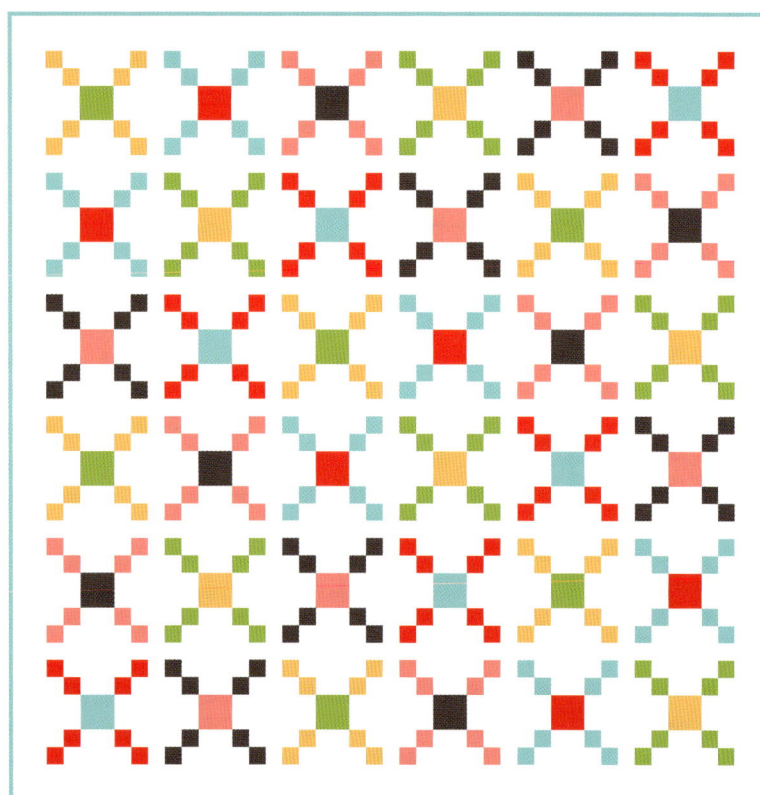

90 ½" x 90 ½"

CUTTING INSTRUCTIONS:

One Layer Cake (36 - 10" squares)	
Blocks 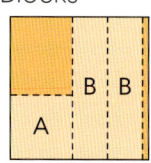	From each 10" square cut: 1 - 4 ½" square (A) 2 - 2 ½" x 10" rectangles (B)

6 ½ yards	
Background, Sashing & Borders	18 - 4 ½" x WOF strips, subcut into: 144 - 4 ½" squares (C)
	28 - 2 ½" x WOF strips, subcut into: 30 - 2 ½" x 12 ½" rectangles (D) 72 - 2 ½" x 10" rectangles (E)
	12 - 2 ½" x WOF strips, sew end to end and subcut into: 5 - 2 ½" x 82 ½" strips (F)
	10 - 4 ½" x WOF strips, sew end to end and subcut into: 2 - 4 ½" x 82 ½" strips (G1) 2 - 4 ½" x 90 ½" strips (G2)

⅞ yard	
Binding	10 - 2 ½" x WOF strips (H)

| 8 ⅜ yards Backing | |

Coffee Quilt

COFFEE BLOCKS:

Each Block uses two 10" squares (pair).

Assemble one Fabric B rectangle and one Fabric E rectangle.
Strip Set should measure 4 ½" x 10".

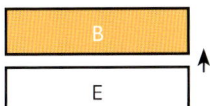

Make two from each 10" square.
Make seventy-two total.

Subcut each Strip Set into four 2 ½" x 4 ½" rectangles.
Partial Four Patch Unit should measure 2 ½" x 4 ½".

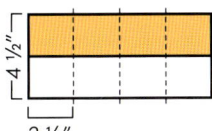 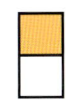

Make eight from each 10" square.
Make two hundred eighty-eight total.

Assemble Unit using matching fabric.
Four Patch Unit should measure 4 ½" x 4 ½".

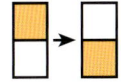

Make four from each 10" square.
Make one hundred forty-four total.

Assemble Block using coordinating fabric.
Coffee Block should measure 12 ½" x 12 ½".

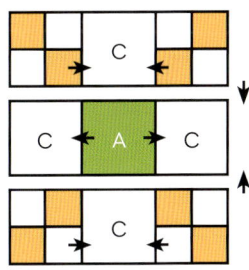 

Make two from each pair.
Make thirty-six total.

Coffee Quilt

QUILT CENTER:

Assemble Quilt Center. Press toward the Fabric D rectangles.

Quilt Center should measure 82 ½" x 82 ½".

BORDERS:

Attach the Side Borders using the Fabric G1 strips.

Attach the Top and Bottom Borders using the Fabric G2 strips.

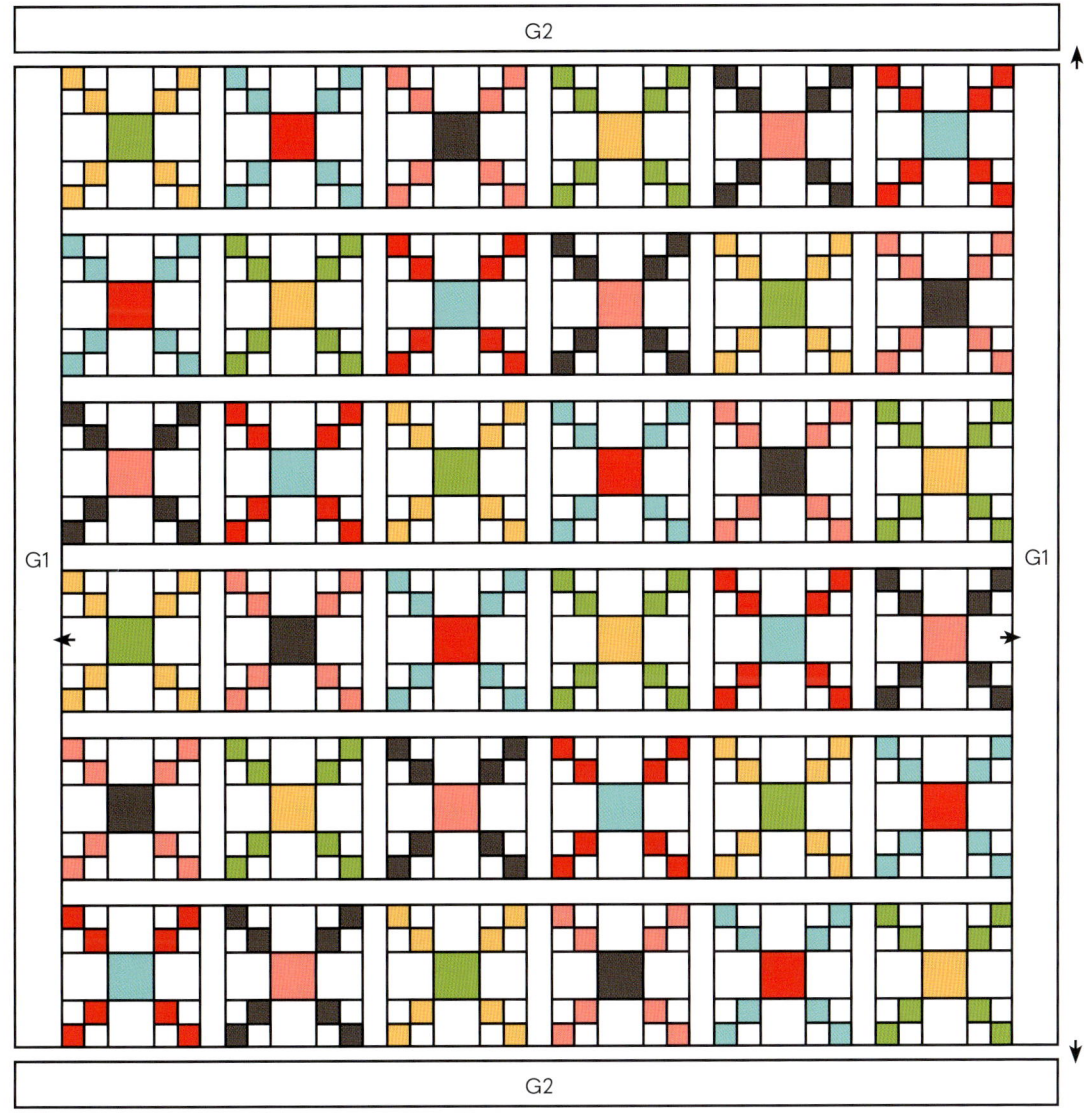

FINISHING:

Piece the Fabric H strips end to end for binding.

Quilt and bind as desired.

Cookie Dough Quilt

88 ½" x 88 ½"

CUTTING INSTRUCTIONS:

One Layer Cake (36 - 10" squares)	
Blocks 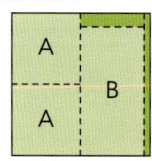	From each 10" square cut: 2 - 5" squares (A) 1 - 4 ½" x 9" rectangle (B)

5 ⅞ yards	
Background, Sashing & Borders	9 - 5" x WOF strips, subcut into: 72 - 5" squares (C)
	14 - 4 ½" x WOF strips, subcut into: 36 - 4 ½" x 9" rectangles (D) 36 - 4 ½" squares (E)
	6 - 4 ½" x WOF strips, subcut into: 6 - 4 ½" x 24 ½" strips (F)
	15 - 4 ½" x WOF strips, sew end to end and subcut into: 2 - 4 ½" x 80 ½" strips (G1) 2 - 4 ½" x 80 ½" strips (G2) 2 - 4 ½" x 88 ½" strips (G3)

⅞ yard	
Binding	10 - 2 ½" x WOF strips (H)

| 8 ¼ yards Backing |

Cookie Dough Quilt

COOKIE DOUGH BLOCKS:

Each Block uses four 10" squares (set).

Draw a diagonal line on the wrong side of the Fabric C squares.

With right sides facing, layer a Fabric C square with a Fabric A square.

Stitch ¼" from each side of the drawn line.

Cut apart on the marked line.

TRIM Half Square Triangle Unit to measure 4 ½" x 4 ½".

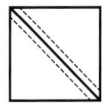  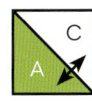

Make four from each 10" square.

Make one hundred forty-four total.

Assemble one Fabric B rectangle and one Fabric D rectangle.

Strip Set should measure 8 ½" x 9".

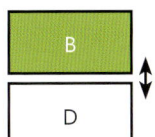 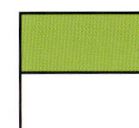

Make one from each 10" square.

Make thirty-six total.

Subcut each Strip Set into two 4 ½" x 8 ½" rectangles.

Partial Four Patch Unit should measure 4 ½" x 8 ½".

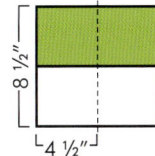 

Make two from each 10" square.

Make seventy-two total.

Assemble Unit using matching fabric.

Four Patch Unit should measure 8 ½" x 8 ½".

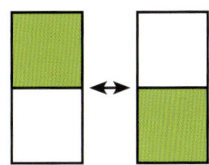 

Make one from each 10" square.

Make thirty-six total.

Assemble Unit using matching fabric.

Cookie Dough Unit should measure 12 ½" x 12 ½".

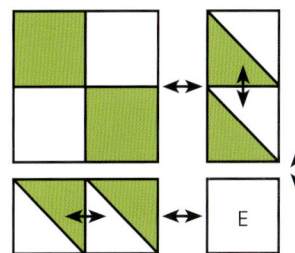 

Make one from each 10" square.

Make thirty-six total.

Assemble Block using coordinating fabric.

Cookie Dough Block should measure 24 ½" x 24 ½".

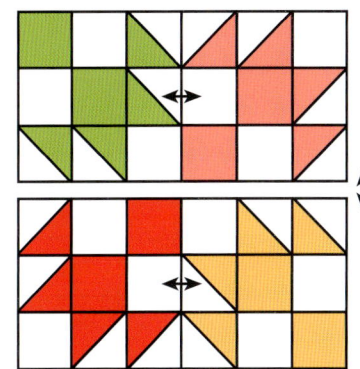 

Make one from each set.

Make nine total.

Cookie Dough Quilt

QUILT CENTER:

Assemble Quilt Center. Press toward the Fabric F strips.

Quilt Center should measure 80 ½" x 80 ½".

BORDERS:

Attach the Side Borders using the Fabric G2 strips.

Attach the Top and Bottom Borders using the Fabric G3 strips.

FINISHING:

Piece the Fabric H strips end to end for binding.

Quilt and bind as desired.

Cookies 'n Cream Quilt

60 ½" x 60 ½"

CUTTING INSTRUCTIONS:

One Layer Cake (32 - 10" squares)	
Blocks 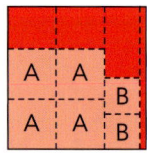	From each 10" square cut: 4 - 3 ½" squares (A) 2 - 2 ½" squares (B)

3 ⅜ yards	
Background, Sashing & Borders	13 - 3 ½" x WOF strips, subcut into: 128 - 3 ½" squares (C)
	12 - 2 ½" x WOF strips, subcut into: 12 - 2 ½" x 12 ½" rectangles (D) 64 - 2 ½" x 3 ½" rectangles (E) 16 - 2 ½" squares (F)
	5 - 2 ½" x WOF strips, sew end to end and subcut into: 3 - 2 ½" x 54 ½" strips (G)
	7 - 3 ½" x WOF strips, sew end to end and subcut into: 2 - 3 ½" x 54 ½" strips (H1) 2 - 3 ½" x 60 ½" strips (H2)

⅝ yard	
Binding	7 - 2 ½" x WOF strips (I)

| 4 yards Backing | |

Cookies 'n Cream Quilt

COOKIES 'N CREAM BLOCKS:

Each Block uses two 10" squares (pair).

Draw a diagonal line on the wrong side of the Fabric C squares.

With right sides facing, layer a Fabric C square with a Fabric A square.

Stitch ¼" from each side of the drawn line.

Cut apart on the marked line.

TRIM Half Square Triangle Unit to measure 3" x 3".

Make eight from each 10" square.

Make two hundred fifty-six total.

Assemble Unit using matching fabric.

Cookies 'n Cream Unit should measure 5 ½" x 5 ½".

Make two from each 10" square.

Make sixty-four total.

Assemble Unit.

Middle Unit should measure 2 ½" x 5 ½".

Make two from each 10" square.

Make sixty-four total.

Assemble Block using coordinating fabric.

Cookies 'n Cream Block should measure 12 ½" x 12 ½".

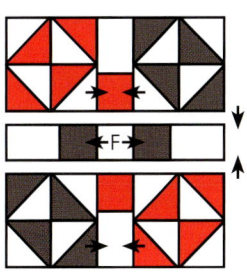 

Make one from each pair.

Make sixteen total.

PERFECT 10 QUILTS   29

Cookies 'n Cream Quilt

QUILT CENTER:

Assemble Quilt Center. Press toward the Fabric D rectangles.

Quilt Center should measure 54 ½" x 54 ½".

BORDERS:

Attach the Side Borders using the Fabric H1 strips.

Attach the Top and Bottom Borders using the Fabric H2 strips.

FINISHING:

Piece the Fabric I strips end to end for binding.

Quilt and bind as desired.

Cotton Candy Quilt

65 ½" x 65 ½"

CUTTING INSTRUCTIONS:

One Layer Cake (36 - 10" squares)	
Blocks 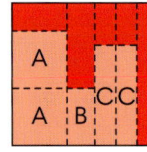	From each 10" square cut: 2 - 4" squares (A) 1 - 2" x 4" rectangle (B) 2 - 1 ½" x 7" rectangles (C)

4 yards	
Background, Sashing & Borders	8 - 4" x WOF strips, subcut into: 72 - 4" squares (D)
	4 - 2" x WOF strips, subcut into: 36 - 2" x 4" rectangles (E)
	37 - 1 ½" x WOF strips, subcut into: 30 - 1 ½" x 9 ½" rectangles (F) 144 - 1 ½" x 7" rectangles (G)
	8 - 1 ½" x WOF strips, sew end to end and subcut into: 5 - 1 ½" x 59 ½" strips (H)
	8 - 3 ½" x WOF strips, sew end to end and subcut into: 2 - 3 ½" x 59 ½" strips (I1) 2 - 3 ½" x 65 ½" strips (I2)

¾ yard	
Binding	8 - 2 ½" x WOF strips (J)

| 4 ¼ yards Backing | |

Cotton Candy Quilt

COTTON CANDY BLOCKS:

Draw a diagonal line on the wrong side of the Fabric D squares.

With right sides facing, layer a Fabric D square with a Fabric A square.

Stitch ¼" from each side of the drawn line.

Cut apart on the marked line.

TRIM Half Square Triangle Unit to measure 3 ½" x 3 ½".

Make four from each 10" square.

Make one hundred forty-four total.

Assemble two Fabric G rectangles and one Fabric C rectangle.

Middle Strip Set should measure 3 ½" x 7".

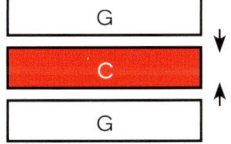 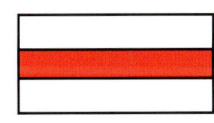

Make two from each 10" square.

Make seventy-two total.

Subcut each Middle Strip Set into two 3 ½" squares.

Three Patch Unit should measure 3 ½" x 3 ½".

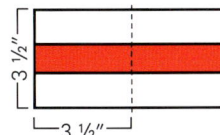 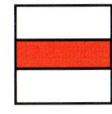

Make four from each 10" square.

Make one hundred forty-four total.

Assemble one Fabric B rectangle and one Fabric E rectangle.

Center Strip Set should measure 3 ½" x 4".

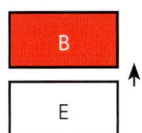 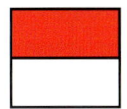

Make one from each 10" square.

Make thirty-six total.

Subcut each Center Strip Set into two 2" x 3 ½" rectangles.

Partial Four Patch Unit should measure 2" x 3 ½".

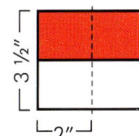 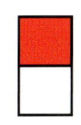

Make two from each 10" square.

Make seventy-two total.

Assemble Unit using matching fabric.

Four Patch Unit should measure 3 ½" x 3 ½".

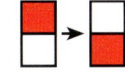

Make one from each 10" square.

Make thirty-six total.

Assemble Block using matching fabric.

Cotton Candy Block should measure 9 ½" x 9 ½".

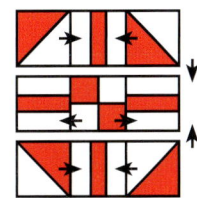 

Make one from each 10" square.

Make thirty-six total.

Cotton Candy Quilt

QUILT CENTER:

Assemble Quilt Center. Press toward the Fabric F rectangles.

Quilt Center should measure 59 ½" x 59 ½".

Cotton Candy Quilt

BORDERS:

Attach the Side Borders using the Fabric I1 strips.

Attach the Top and Bottom Borders using the Fabric I2 strips.

FINISHING:

Piece the Fabric J strips end to end for binding.

Quilt and bind as desired.

PERFECT 10 QUILTS

Dutch Chocolate Quilt

65" x 84 ½"

CUTTING INSTRUCTIONS:

One Print Layer Cake (36 - 10" squares)	
Blocks 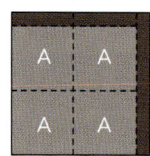	From each 10" square cut: 4 - 4 ½" squares (A)

One Solid Layer Cake (36 - 10" squares)	
Blocks 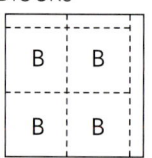	From each 10" square cut: 4 - 4 ½" squares (B)

2 ¼ yards	
Background, Sashing & Borders	2 - 4" x WOF strips, subcut into: 12 - 4" squares (C)
	4 - 2 ½" x WOF strips, subcut into: 8 - 2 ½" x 18" rectangles (D)
	5 - 2 ½" x WOF strips, sew end to end and subcut into: 3 - 2 ½" x 57" strips (E)
	9 - 4 ½" x WOF strips, sew end to end and subcut into: 2 - 4 ½" x 76 ½" strips (F1) 2 - 4 ½" x 65" strips (F2)

⅞ yard	
Binding	9 - 2 ½" x WOF strips (G)

| 5 ¼ yards Backing | |

Dutch Chocolate Quilt

DUTCH CHOCOLATE BLOCKS:

Each Block uses three 10" print squares (set).

Draw a diagonal line on the wrong side of the Fabric B squares.

With right sides facing, layer a Fabric B square with a Fabric A square.

Stitch ¼" from each side of the drawn line.

Cut apart on the marked line.

TRIM Half Square Triangle Unit to measure 4" x 4".

Make eight from each 10" print square.

Make two hundred eighty-eight total.

Assemble Unit using coordinating fabric.

Large Dutch Chocolate Unit should measure 7 ½" x 7 ½".

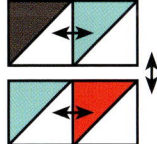 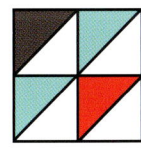

Make four from each set.

Make forty-eight total.

Assemble Unit using coordinating fabric.

Small Dutch Chocolate One Unit should measure 4" x 7 ½".

Make two from each set.

Make twenty-four total.

Assemble Unit using coordinating fabric.

Small Dutch Chocolate Two Unit should measure 4" x 7 ½".

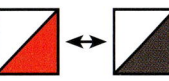 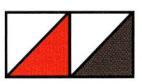

Make two from each set.

Make twenty-four total.

Assemble Block using coordinating fabric.

Dutch Chocolate Block should measure 18" x 18".

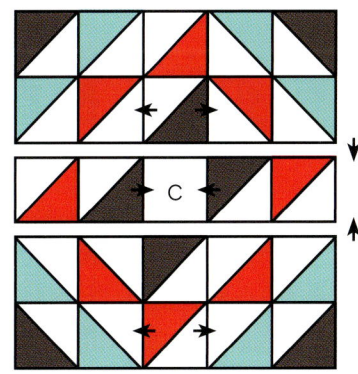 

Make one from each set.

Make twelve total.

PERFECT 10 QUILTS 37

Dutch Chocolate Quilt

QUILT CENTER:

Assemble Quilt Center. Press toward the Fabric D rectangles.

Quilt Center should measure 57" x 76 ½".

BORDERS:

Attach the Side Borders using the Fabric F1 strips.

Attach the Top and Bottom Borders using the Fabric F2 strips.

FINISHING:

Piece the Fabric G strips end to end for binding.

Quilt and bind as desired.

French Vanilla Quilt

66 ½" x 78 ½"

CUTTING INSTRUCTIONS:

One Layer Cake (30 - 10" squares)	
Blocks 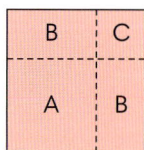	From each 10" square cut: 1 - 6 ½" square (A) 2 - 3 ½" x 6 ½" rectangles (B) 1 - 3 ½" square (C)
3 ⅛ yards	

Background, Sashing & Borders	17 - 1 ½" x WOF strips, subcut into:
	  30 - 1 ½" x 10 ½" rectangles (D)
	  30 - 1 ½" x 6 ½" rectangles (E)
	  30 - 1 ½" x 3 ½" rectangles (F)
	8 - 2 ½" x WOF strips, subcut into:
	  24 - 2 ½" x 10 ½" rectangles (G)
	8 - 2 ½" x WOF strips, sew end to end and subcut into:
	  5 - 2 ½" x 58 ½" strips (H)
	8 - 4 ½" x WOF strips, sew end to end and subcut into:
	  2 - 4 ½" x 70 ½" strips (I1)
	  2 - 4 ½" x 66 ½" strips (I2)

¾ yard	
Binding	8 - 2 ½" x WOF strips (J)
5 yards Backing	

French Vanilla Quilt

FRENCH VANILLA BLOCKS:

Blocks are intended to be scrappy.

Assemble Unit.

Small French Vanilla Unit should measure 3 ½" x 10 ½".

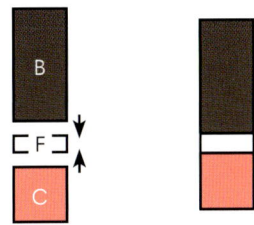

Make thirty total.

Assemble Unit.

Large French Vanilla Unit should measure 6 ½" x 10 ½".

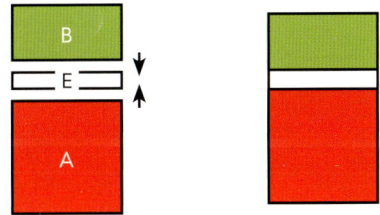

Make thirty total.

Assemble Block.

French Vanilla Block should measure 10 ½" x 10 ½".

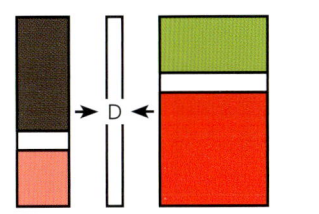

Make thirty total.

PERFECT 10 QUILTS

French Vanilla Quilt

QUILT CENTER:

Assemble Quilt Center. Press toward the Fabric G rectangles.

Quilt Center should measure 58 ½" x 70 ½".

French Vanilla Quilt

BORDERS:

Attach the Side Borders using the Fabric I1 strips.

Attach the Top and Bottom Borders using the Fabric I2 strips.

FINISHING:

Piece the Fabric J strips end to end for binding.

Quilt and bind as desired.

Lemon Sorbet Quilt

91 ½" x 91 ½"

CUTTING INSTRUCTIONS:

One Print Layer Cake (36 - 10" squares)	
Blocks 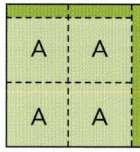	From each 10" square cut: 4 - 4 ½" squares (A)
One Solid Layer Cake (36 - 10" squares)	
Blocks 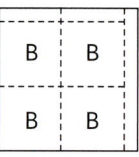	From each 10" square cut: 4 - 4 ½" squares (B)
5 ⅓ yards	
Background & Borders	36 - 4" x WOF strips, subcut into: 72 - 4" x 14 ½" rectangles (C) 10 - 4" x WOF strips, sew end to end and subcut into: 2 - 4" x 84 ½" strips (D1) 2 - 4" x 91 ½" strips (D2)
⅞ yard	
Binding	10 - 2 ½" x WOF strips (E)
8 ½ yards Backing	

Lemon Sorbet Quilt

LEMON SORBET BLOCKS:

Each Block uses two 10" print squares (pair).

Draw a diagonal line on the wrong side of the Fabric B squares.

With right sides facing, layer a Fabric B square with a Fabric A square.

Stitch ¼" from each side of the drawn line.

Cut apart on the marked line.

TRIM Half Square Triangle Unit to measure 4" x 4".

Make eight from each 10" print square.

Make two hundred eighty-eight total.

Assemble Unit using coordinating fabric.

Lemon Sorbet Unit should measure 7 ½" x 7 ½".

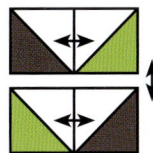 

Make four from each pair.

Make seventy-two total.

Assemble Block using coordinating fabric.

Lemon Sorbet Block should measure 14 ½" x 14 ½".

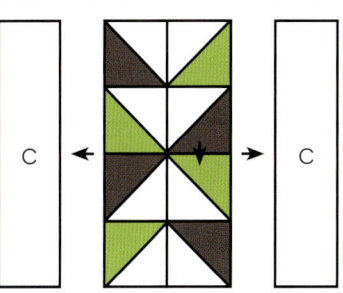 

Make two from each pair.

Make thirty-six total.

Lemon Sorbet Quilt

QUILT CENTER:

Assemble Quilt Center. Press rows in opposite directions.

Quilt Center should measure 84 ½" x 84 ½".

BORDERS:

Attach the Side Borders using the Fabric D1 strips.

Attach the Top and Bottom Borders using the Fabric D2 strips.

FINISHING:

Piece the Fabric E strips end to end for binding.

Quilt and bind as desired.

PERFECT 10 QUILTS

Mint Chocolate Chip Quilt

78 ½" x 78 ½"

CUTTING INSTRUCTIONS:

One Print Layer Cake (32 - 10" squares)	
Blocks 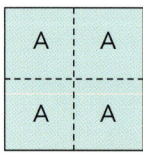	From each 10" square cut: 4 - 5" squares (A)
One Solid Layer Cake (32 - 10" squares)	
Blocks 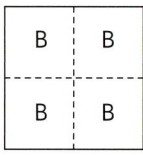	From each 10" square cut: 4 - 5" squares (B)
2 ¼ yards	
Background, Sashing & Borders	6 - 2 ½" x WOF strips, subcut into: 12 - 2 ½" x 16 ½" rectangles (C)
	6 - 2 ½" x WOF strips, sew end to end and subcut into: 3 - 2 ½" x 70 ½" strips (D)
	9 - 4 ½" x WOF strips, sew end to end and subcut into: 2 - 4 ½" x 70 ½" strips (E1) 2 - 4 ½" x 78 ½" strips (E2)
⅞ yard	
Binding	9 - 2 ½" x WOF strips (F)
7 ⅜ yards Backing	

Mint Chocolate Chip Quilt

MINT CHOCOLATE CHIP BLOCKS:

Each Block uses two 10" print squares (pair).

Draw a diagonal line on the wrong side of the Fabric B squares.

With right sides facing, layer a Fabric B square with a Fabric A square.

Stitch ¼" from each side of the drawn line.

Cut apart on the marked line.

TRIM Half Square Triangle Unit to measure 4 ½" x 4 ½".

 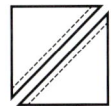 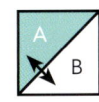

Make eight from each 10" print square.

Make two hundred fifty-six total.

Assemble Unit using matching fabric.

Mint Chocolate Chip Unit should measure 8 ½" x 8 ½".

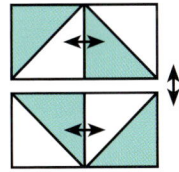 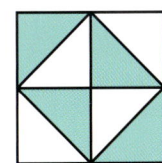

Make two from each 10" print square.

Make sixty-four total.

Assemble Block using coordinating fabric.

Mint Chocolate Chip Block One should measure 16 ½" x 16 ½".

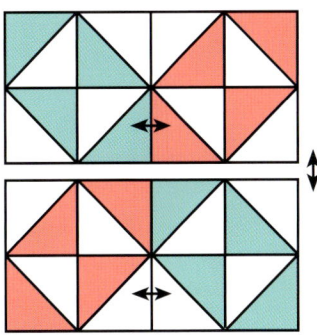 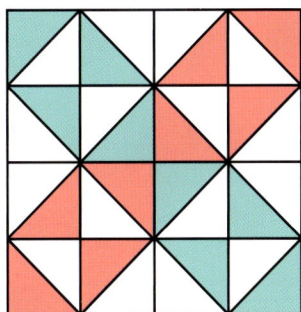

Make eight total.

Assemble Block using coordinating fabric.

Mint Chocolate Chip Block Two should measure 16 ½" x 16 ½".

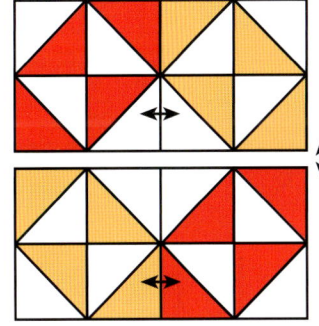 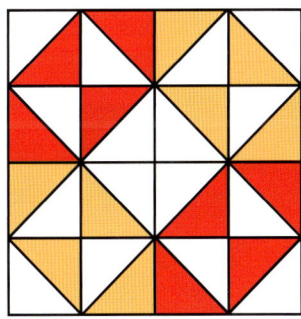

Make eight total.

Mint Chocolate Chip Quilt

QUILT CENTER:

Assemble Quilt Center. Press toward the Fabric C rectangles.

Quilt Center should measure 70 ½" x 70 ½".

Mint Chocolate Chip Quilt

BORDERS:

Attach the Side Borders using the Fabric E1 strips.

Attach the Top and Bottom Borders using the Fabric E2 strips.

FINISHING:

Piece the Fabric F strips end to end for binding.

Quilt and bind as desired.

Neapolitan Quilt

58 ½" x 70 ½"

CUTTING INSTRUCTIONS:

One Layer Cake (33 - 10" squares)	
Blocks 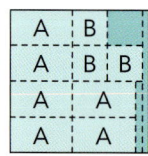	From each 10" square cut: 6 - 2 ½" x 4 ½" rectangles (A) 3 - 2 ½" squares (B)

4 ⅜ yards	
Background & Borders	25 - 2 ½" x WOF strips, subcut into: 396 - 2 ½" squares (C)
	46 - 1 ½" x WOF strips, subcut into: 198 - 1 ½" x 6 ½" rectangles (D) 198 - 1 ½" x 2 ½" rectangles (E)
	7 - 2 ½" x WOF strips, sew end to end and subcut into: 2 - 2 ½" x 66 ½" strips (F1) 2 - 2 ½" x 58 ½" strips (F2)

¾ yard	
Binding	8 - 2 ½" x WOF strips (G)

| 3 ⅞ yards Backing | |

Neapolitan Quilt

NEAPOLITAN BLOCKS:

Draw a diagonal line on the wrong side of the Fabric C squares.

With right sides facing, layer a Fabric C square on the top end of a Fabric A rectangle.

Stitch on the drawn line and trim ¼" away from the seam.

Repeat on the bottom end.

Flying Geese Unit should measure 2 ½" x 4 ½".

Make six from each 10" square.

Make one hundred ninety-eight total.

Assemble Unit using matching fabric.

Neapolitan Unit should measure 4 ½" x 6 ½".

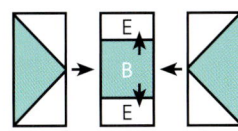 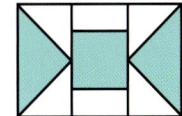

Make three from each 10" square.

Make ninety-nine total.

Assemble Block.

Neapolitan Block should measure 6 ½" x 6 ½".

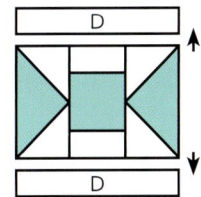 

Make three from each 10" square.

Make ninety-nine total.

PERFECT 10 QUILTS 53

Neapolitan Quilt

QUILT CENTER:

Assemble Quilt Center. Press rows in opposite directions.

Quilt Center should measure 54 ½" x 66 ½".

BORDERS:

Attach the Side Borders using the Fabric F1 strips.

Attach the Top and Bottom Borders using the Fabric F2 strips.

FINISHING:

Piece the Fabric G strips end to end for binding.

Quilt and bind as desired.

Peaches 'n Cream Quilt

64 ½" x 64 ½"

CUTTING INSTRUCTIONS:

One Layer Cake (36 - 10" squares)	
Blocks 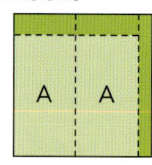	From each 10" square cut: 2 - 4 ½" x 8 ½" rectangles (A)
4 ¼ yards	
Background, Sashing & Borders	21 - 4 ½" x WOF strips, subcut into: 6 - 4 ½" x 16 ½" rectangles (B) 144 - 4 ½" squares (C)
	11 - 4 ½" x WOF strips, sew end to end and subcut into: 2 - 4 ½" x 56 ½" strips (D1) 2 - 4 ½" x 56 ½" strips (D2) 2 - 4 ½" x 64 ½" strips (D3)
¾ yard	
Binding	8 - 2 ½" x WOF strips (E)
4 ¼ yards Backing	

Peaches 'n Cream Quilt

PEACHES 'N CREAM BLOCKS:

Each Block uses four 10" squares (set).

Draw a diagonal line on the wrong side of the Fabric C squares.

With right sides facing, layer a Fabric C square on one end of a Fabric A rectangle.

Stitch on the drawn line and trim ¼" away from the seam.

 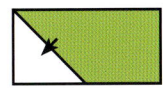

Repeat on the opposite end.

Flying Geese Unit should measure 4 ½" x 8 ½".

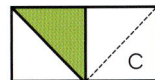 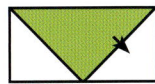

Make two from each 10" square.

Make seventy-two total.

Assemble Unit using coordinating fabric.

Peaches 'n Cream Unit should measure 8 ½" x 8 ½".

 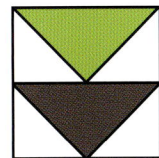

Make four from each set.

Make thirty-six total.

Assemble Block using coordinating fabric.

Peaches 'n Cream Block should measure 16 ½" x 16 ½".

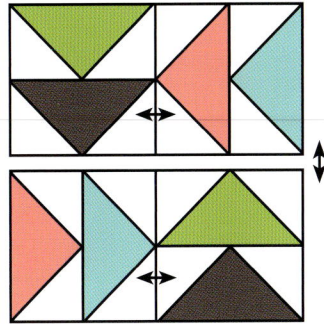 

Make one from each set.

Make nine total.

PERFECT 10 QUILTS 57

Peaches 'n Cream Quilt

QUILT CENTER:

Assemble Quilt Center. Press toward the Fabric B rectangles.

Quilt Center should measure 56 ½" x 56 ½".

Peaches 'n Cream Quilt

BORDERS:

Attach the Side Borders using the Fabric D2 strips.

Attach the Top and Bottom Borders using the Fabric D3 strips.

FINISHING:

Piece the Fabric E strips end to end for binding.

Quilt and bind as desired.

PERFECT 10 QUILTS

Rainbow Sherbet Quilt

84 ½" x 84 ½"

CUTTING INSTRUCTIONS:

One Layer Cake (36 - 10" squares)	
Blocks 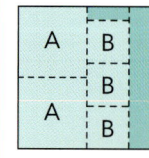	From each 10" square cut: 2 - 5" squares (A) 3 - 3" squares (B)

6 ¼ yards	
Background, Sashing & Borders	9 - 8 ½" x WOF strips, subcut into: 36 - 8 ½" squares (C)
	9 - 5" x WOF strips, subcut into: 72 - 5" squares (D)
	5 - 4 ½" x WOF strips, subcut into: 36 - 4 ½" squares (E)
	6 - 3 ½" x WOF strips, subcut into: 6 - 3 ½" x 24 ½" strips (F)
	14 - 3 ½" x WOF strips, sew end to end and subcut into: 2 - 3 ½" x 78 ½" strips (G1) 2 - 3 ½" x 78 ½" strips (G2) 2 - 3 ½" x 84 ½" strips (G3)

⅞ yard	
Binding	10 - 2 ½" x WOF strips (H)

| 7 ⅞ yards Backing | |

RAINBOW SHERBET BLOCKS:

Each Block uses four 10" squares (set).

Draw a diagonal line on the wrong side of the Fabric D squares.

With right sides facing, layer a Fabric D square with a Fabric A square.

Stitch ¼" from each side of the drawn line.

Cut apart on the marked line.

TRIM Half Square Triangle Unit to measure 4 ½" x 4 ½".

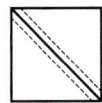  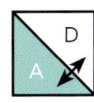

Make four from each 10" square.

Make one hundred forty-four total.

Draw a diagonal line on the wrong side of the Fabric B squares.

With right sides facing, layer a Fabric B square on the top right corner of a Fabric C square.

Stitch on the drawn line and trim ¼" away from the seam.

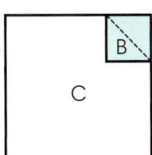 

Repeat on the bottom left and bottom right corners with matching fabric.

Partial Rainbow Sherbet Unit should measure 8 ½" x 8 ½".

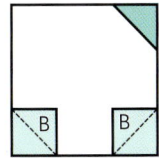 

Make one from each 10" square.

Make thirty-six total.

Assemble Unit using matching fabric.

Rainbow Sherbet Unit should measure 12 ½" x 12 ½".

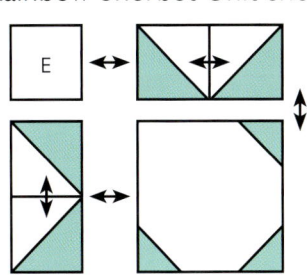 

Make one from each 10" square.

Make thirty-six total.

Assemble Block using coordinating fabric.

Rainbow Sherbet Block should measure 24 ½" x 24 ½".

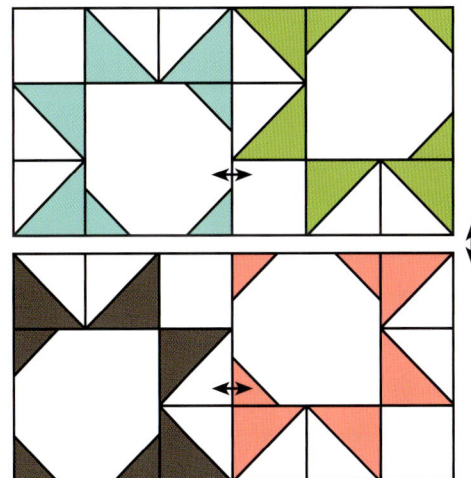

Make one from each set.

Make nine total.

Rainbow Sherbet Quilt

QUILT CENTER:

Assemble Quilt Center. Press toward the Fabric F strips.

Quilt Center should measure 78 ½" x 78 ½".

BORDERS:

Attach the Side Borders using the Fabric G2 strips.

Attach the Top and Bottom Borders using the Fabric G3 strips.

FINISHING:

Piece the Fabric H strips end to end for binding.

Quilt and bind as desired.

Rocky Road Quilt

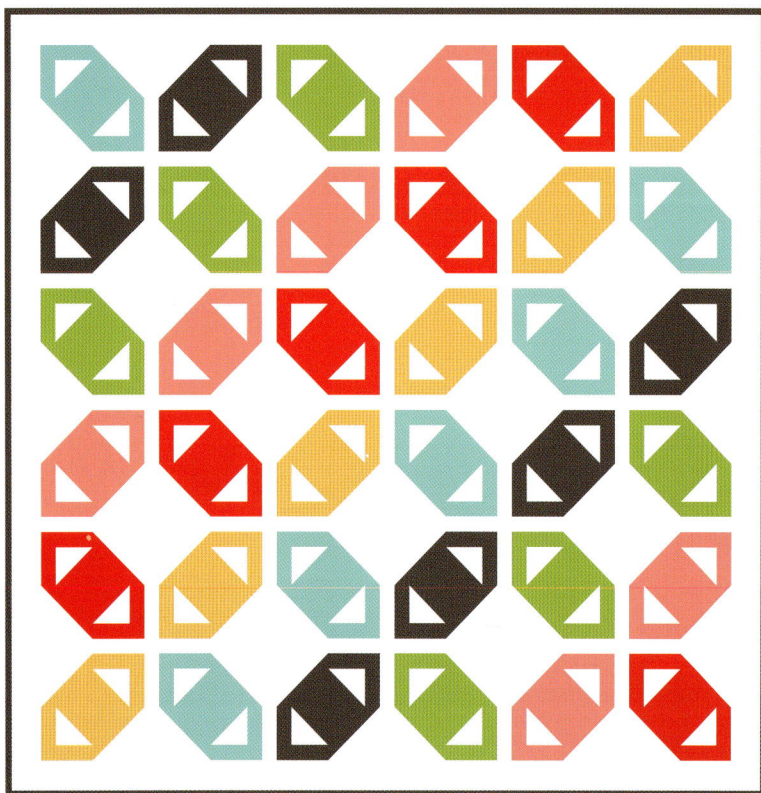

66 ½" x 66 ½"

CUTTING INSTRUCTIONS:

One Layer Cake (36 - 10" squares)	
Blocks 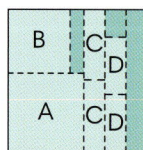	From each 10" square cut: 1 - 5 ½" square (A) 1 - 4 ½" square (B) 2 - 1 ½" x 5" rectangles (C) 2 - 1 ½" x 4" rectangles (D)
3 ⅓ yards	
Background, Sashing & Borders	6 - 5 ½" x WOF strips, subcut into: 36 - 5 ½" squares (E)
	5 - 4 ½" x WOF strips, subcut into: 36 - 4 ½" squares (F)
	8 - 1 ½" x WOF strips, subcut into: 30 - 1 ½" x 9 ½" rectangles (G)
	8 - 1 ½" x WOF strips, sew end to end and subcut into: 5 - 1 ½" x 59 ½" strips (H)
	8 - 4" x WOF strips, sew end to end and subcut into: 2 - 4" x 59 ½" strips (I1) 2 - 4" x 66 ½" strips (I2)
¾ yard	
Binding	8 - 2 ½" x WOF strips (J)
4 ¼ yards Backing	

Rocky Road Quilt

ROCKY ROAD BLOCKS:

Draw a diagonal line on the wrong side of the Fabric E squares.

With right sides facing, layer a Fabric E square with a Fabric A square.

Stitch ¼" from each side of the drawn line.

Cut apart on the marked line.

TRIM Large Half Square Triangle Unit to measure 5" x 5".

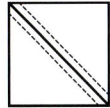  

Make two from each 10" square.

Make seventy-two total.

- -

Draw a diagonal line on the wrong side of the Fabric F squares.

With right sides facing, layer a Fabric F square with a Fabric B square.

Stitch ¼" from each side of the drawn line.

Cut apart on the marked line.

TRIM Small Half Square Triangle Unit to measure 4" x 4".

 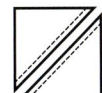

Make two from each 10" square.

Make seventy-two total.

Assemble Unit using matching fabric.

Rocky Road Unit should measure 5" x 5".

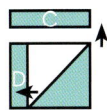

Make two from each 10" square.

Make seventy-two total.

- -

Assemble Block using matching fabric.

Rocky Road Block should measure 9 ½" x 9 ½".

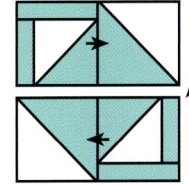 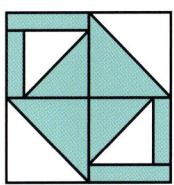

Make one from each 10" square.

Make thirty-six total.

PERFECT 10 QUILTS 65

Rocky Road Quilt

QUILT CENTER:

Assemble Quilt Center. Press toward the Fabric G rectangles.

Quilt Center should measure 59 ½" x 59 ½".

PERFECT 10 QUILTS